Connecting Entrepreneurs, Philanthropists and Influencers.

BUSINESS

BOOSTER TODAY MAGAZINE

THE #1 GERMANY BASED MAGAZINE FOR THE GLOBAL ENTREPRENEUR

THE PIPER M600 | P.6

I0494566

VOL. 2 | NO.4 | APR2019

CONTENT

SECTIONS

FOUNDER'S CORNER

By Sue Baumgärtner-Bartsch & Christian Bartsch

The Business Booster Today Magazine is currently transitioning into its 3rd phase of development.

Online Team Growth

The online magazine is being expanded by an additional journalist team that will contribute to the articles we **publish** on a **daily** base. These contributing writers are now working on essays and reports on all sorts of business related topics.

Section teams and Leaders

Furthermore, you will experience a change in our **editorial team structure** as the online teams and the print teams will have overlapping team members.

Entrepreneurs from Europe, North America and Asia are also contributing to the introduction of our magazine to **key players** in the various industries.

This makes it necessary to have for each topic section a team leader. the property section is lead by **John Stokoe**, a seasoned property investor based in the United Kingdom.

Magazine Advisory Board

Our magazine will set up an advisory board consisting of entrepreneurs, coaches and journalists who will **provide wisdom to the publisher** of the magazine.

Some of these entrepreneurs have been in business for over 50 years. They are based in Europe, USA, Canada, Singapore, Germany and the United Kingdom.

Topic Expansion

The magazine is now expanding its topics towards areas such as Environment, Aircraft, Export, Infrastructure, Leadership and other topics.

Therefore the contributing writers and editors of the Business Booster Today Magazine are present at exhibitions around the world.

Cooperation Expansion

The cooperation with the US based magazine "Heart of Hollywood" has proven to be a positive move. This is the reason for next months announcement of a further cooperation agreement for another magazine overseas.

Airline & Lounges

Our magazine is now available through the e-Journal system in various **airlines**, such as Lufthansa, Swiss, Eurowings and Austrian. You can also download the magazine from the system in the SWISS business lounges in Zurich and Geneva.

Hotel Introductions

Next months editions will start introducing some of the Hotels that provide access to our magazine. You will be astonished which beautiful destinations are waiting for you. ✈

EDITORIAL PANEL

Christian Bartsch
Publisher/Chief E.

Sue Baumgärtner-Bartsch
Lead Interviewer.

Udo Bartsch
Editor (Germany)

John Stokoe
Editor (UK)

Eren Ünlü
Editor (Germany)

Jan Erik Horgen
Editor (Norway)

Aldrin-David Verburgt
Stylist (Netherlands)

Michael Knulst
Editor (Netherlands)

Marina Kotze
Editor (South Africa)

Louis Kotze
Editor (South Africa)

Stefanos Sifandos
Editor (USA)

Melody Garcia
Editor (USA)

Jim Paar
Editor (USA)

IMPRESS

ISSN (Print Edition)

2627-9223

ISSN (Online Edition)

2627-9231

PUBLICATION DATE

23.04.2019

PUBLICATION SERIES INFO

April 2019 No. 4

PUBLICATION REVISION ID

2021-05-28--1

PUBLISHER & EDITOR IN CHIEF

Christian Bartsch

LEAD EDITOR & VP

Sue Baumgaertner-Bartsch

CONTRIBUTING EDITORS

Udo Bartsch, Douglas Vermeeren, Jan Erik Horgen, Michael Knulst, Louis Kotze, Sylvija Popovic, John Stokoe, Eren Ünlü, Greg JC Granier

CONTRIBUTING WRITERS

Michelle Davis, Robb Evans, Billy Gajic, Raluca Gomeaja, Marina Kotze, Sam Komeha, Kati Israel, Jaine Lopez, Milos & Danijela Nakovski, Peutherer, Richard Peutherer, Gavin Sim, Nina Schmid, Kirstie Shapiro, Tomer Sapir Spitkowski, Cristina Stavinski, Mona Tenjo, Janine Van Throo, Yasemin Yazan, Brett Yeager, Erwin Wils, Sabine Zettl

PHOTOGRAPHY

Dalibor Kojic

VIP STYLING & MAKEUP

Aldrin-David Verburgt

PUBLISHED BY

ACATO GmbH, 1st. Floor, Theresienhoehe 28, 80339 Munich, Germany

ADVERTISING & SALES

sales@businessboostertoday.com

Phone +49 89 54041070

www.businessboostertoday.com

SUBSCRIPTIONS

Booster club members: annual membership dues include €197 for a regular one-year subscription and €47 for an electronic member subscription. Non-members subscription rate are €97 for an electronic subscription. Change of address notices and subscriptions should be directed to BBT magazine.

THE PIPER M600

AERO Friedrichshaven 2019 Report

By Christian Bartsch (Germany)

Introduction

The single-engine Piper M600 was exhibited at the German exhibition AERO Friedrichshafen. The team of the Business Booster Today Magazine had the pleasure to get to explore the beautiful design and interior during this exhibition.

The M600 is more of what you want in luxury, performance and value. Aircraft operators call the Piper M600 the best value in its class. Piper designed the M600 for owners who want extra range and speed without the inflated cost.

The wing is at the heart of the Piper M600 providing slick aerodynamics that help you go farther, faster without leaving anything or anyone behind.

Design

With the M600 Piper Introduces the most comfortable and luxurious interior they have ever put on display.

Outfitted in premium leather with elegant trim throughout the cabin and a completely pilot-focused cockpit. This makes the M600 stylish and most inviting. Our magazine team was pleasantly surprised how comfortable the interior has been made. The value for money at a base selling price of just under US$ 3 million is unbelievable.

The detail of attention paid by Piper designers and engineers to the cabin seating and cockpit area is remarkable.

We took the invitation to step into the inside of this stylish plane for the owner that wants to travel up to 3071 km (1658 nm).

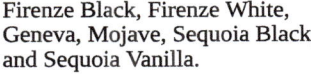

So step into sophistication and enjoy a departure from the ordinary.

The interior of M600 is fashioned in elegance, extraordinary in both feel and function. If this were not enough, Piper provides you the choice of:

Firenze Black, Firenze White, Geneva, Mojave, Sequoia Black, and Sequoia Vanilla.

Safety

The all-glass Garmin G3000 avionics system is a big leap ahead of time. It integrates the most advanced safety technology found in the most modern commercial airliners.

The innovative system produces a multitude of important safety systems. This includes overbanking, under-speed, over-speed protection and emergency descent protection, along with a digitally controlled pressurization system.

No longer does the pilot need to, on approach, sacrifice their scan from the instruments to look down at the approach plate. With 60/40 Mode, all crucial situational information remains right in front of the pilot.

As an additional safety feature,

SurfaceWatch provides aural and visual alerts to help the pilot maintain situational awareness.

Thereby the pilot can avoid potential runway incursions/excursions during ground and air operations in an airport environment.

The Enhanced Map HSI of the Piper M600 is designed to increase situational awareness by overlaying additional information onto the HSI display. Hence, the pilot has a greater ability to keep the situation under control.

Just as the HSI provides the pilot of the Piper M600 increased information compared to the directional gyro, the Enhanced Map HSI further improves the HSI by allowing greater information to be conveyed within the primary instrument scan.

It can be used while in 60/40 Mode and supports overlays with combinations on Map, SafeTaxi, Flight Plan, METARs, NEXRAD, Weather Radar, and more.

Enhanced automatic flight control system

The fully integrated flight control system of the Piper M600 provides exceptional flight automation with a dual AHRS-based system. The system offers top safety features and incomparable performance, seamlessly integrating a flight director, autopilot, automatic trim and yaw damper into the G3000 suite.

The Piper M600's G3000 suite also includes Electronic Stability Protection (ESP), Level Mode, Underspeed Protection (USP), Emergency Descent Mode, and Coupled Go Around, elevating pilot and passenger safety to the highest standards.

Hypoxia recognition system

The standard GTX 33 ES provides ADS-B Out functionality for the Piper M600. ADS-B In can be achieved by adding the optional GTS-825 Traffic Advisory System. The GTS-825 (ADS-B In) traffic systems provide a comprehensive traffic picture.

It can track up to 75 targets within a 40 nm interrogation range. The Piper M600 spoken ATC-like aural alerts help manage your safe flight.

USP of the Piper M600

According to the chart, the Piper M600 comes with a total cost per hour of approx. US$ 900. In contrast the Pilatus PC-12 NG and the Daher TBM930 nearly touch the US$ 1200 mark. The King Air C90GTx barely touches the US$ 1400 barrier.

Looking at the necessary investment to purchase the Piper M600, your budget will be US$ 2,000,000 less than needed for the Pilatus PC-12.

Also, the subject of full fuel load is an important part of the purchase consideration as is at 658 lbs (298 kg). Here the Pilatus is at over a 1000 pounds. The Cessna M2 is a little below that of the payload of the M600.

The maintenance labor cost per hour are also less burden on the maintenance budget.

Pilot Training

The sale of each new Piper M600 comes with a one-week pilot initial, aircraft specific training course. For qualified pilots,

training for the M600 is provided by our exclusive M600 training provider, Legacy Flight Training located at the Piper Factory in Vero Beach, Fl.

The training program combines a thorough academic ground school with aircraft specific training using a full motion flight training device and flight time in the customer's aircraft if needed. ✐

BUILDING AND GROWING BUSINESSES WITH THE RIGHT PEOPLE

By Sue Baumgaertner-Bartsch (Germany)

Some burn contacts in step 1

Life and business are about the people we meet. Nowadays, we have social media, we have Facebook and all these great tools, but what I do not like at all is when people contact me and the first thing, they do is try to sell me something. I am sure you have had this experience too. Or how about when people send you a message and ask what you do via LinkedIn, instead of looking at your profile first **to better understand** what you are doing and to ask an interesting question to start building a relationship?

Build relationships first

We live in a fast-paced world, where people sometimes do not take the time to get to know others at first.

If you want to be successful in business, you need to understand that it takes **9-12 touch points** with **potential customers** before they get to know and trust you and buy from you. That is why your personal branding is so important. Do you know what people say about you when you are not in the room? This is how they see you.

Get to know the person

Show a sincere interest in the other person and get to know them, and **build a relationship**. Think also what you can do for others first. Especially if you meet people who are more successful than you are, refrain from talking about yourself and giving advice.

Successful people could care less about your opinion. Rather ask them questions and get to know the other side. Get to **know their**

interests and hobbies. If you have an opportunity to research them before you meet them, then do so. This will help you start an interesting conversation and will set you apart from the normal and average business people who do not have a clue about the other person and come across as uninformed.

Getting most out of business events

Whenever you go to business events and meetings, find out from the website and the event organizer about the invited guests, or key note speakers. This will help you **be ahead of the game** from all the others who do not take the time to prepare for an event.

No matter what you do: Whether you have an upcoming business meeting, get to meet an influential person, speak in front of an audience or coach people, you want to prepare

yourself.

Preparation is key in everything I do, and I have noted the difference of simply just "showing up" versus **preparing myself ahead** of time. The results are different. You will shine brighter, have deeper conversations and make a greater impact in the lives and businesses of others.

Anticipate what will come

When you prepare, ask yourself what it is that you can bring to the table. Anticipate how your meeting could go and be yourself. You **do not have to know everything**, and it is ok to admit when you do not know something, because that shows you are not a "know-it-all" person, but rather someone who is sincere and authentic.

Ask lots of questions, especially have the other person talk 80% of the time and you only 20% of the time, if the other person is more successful than you are.

Once you have met somebody at an event for example, it does not stop there. You want to build that relationship. And that means, you want to **follow up with that person**.

Successful relationships are all about the follow up and follow throughs! How many people have you met that tell you they will give you a call back and never actually do?

Do not say something and do the opposite thing!

Partners need to be more than just talkers

I highly value sincerity, honesty, integrity and reliability in working with my business partners. I also partner up with A-players. It is important that you understand people and **what drives them**, so that you find the right people to work with you.

If you pay attention to the people around you and the people you meet, you will find that it often takes that **one person to meet and build a relationship with** or that one meeting you go to when new opportunities come your way.

"Business as I say is about the people you meet and the relationships you build. Pay attention to the people you meet and those you want to meet, and always act from a place of authenticity."- Sue Baumgaertner-

Bartsch

Exercise: Make a list of the top 10 people that you want to meet and get to know who you think would be of value to you and your business growth.

It takes on average 4- 5 connections to meet and **get to know that person**. If you think big, you will reach big. If you think it is possible, it will be possible.

Once you have made that list, find out as much as you can about them. Find out, for example, what they read, what the like to do in their free time as a hobby, where these **people socialize and network**, where you can meet them or how to otherwise connect with them. This could be business events, this could be through a social activity or another connection you have.

It takes an **effort and real curiosity** on your part, and time. But imagine you meet that one person that you wanted to meet and then you have your opportunity-that is when you want to show up prepared, ready and able to build that relationship. Go for it! ✒

5 QUESTIONS TO CHECK THE SUCCESS OF YOUR BUSINESS

By Raluca Gomeaja (France)

Success! People may look at success from different angles depending on education, experience, values and much more. When coming to business success there are a few things that may indicate how profitable, value added and sustainable your business really is!

Many strategies have been defined in order to increase business profit, to reduce cost, to take better care of employees!

Yet a shift is happening in the way the world is going, growing and progressing; as its changing at the level of people making business themselves; most of the new graduates which are generally called millenniums are no longer looking at the traditional way of doing business and not very much attracted by traditional corporations; it is no longer only about figures; is how sustainable those figures are and what can define success!

In this **new innovative way of doing business** here are my personal beliefs linked to 5 essential questions to ask in order to make a difference:

1. How successful is your team?

No matter if you are a mid-manager in a corporation or a small size/big size business owner your team will define your success! A successful entrepreneur wants to attract the best!

The question is why the best shall come and work for them? When your team is successful not only you see it in results and the work environment but they are "radiating"/shining outside the business.

Make sure your people are successful; they are your most important capital! You may consider understanding what they think success is, you may consider sharing profit with them, have a team coach to help them grow as a successful team etc. And there are ways to measure it as well!

2. How successful are your clients?

This is probably the oldest definition of success in business: **you don't exist if your clients are not buying what you propose**; why they buy from you: mostly because they need/want what you propose and they are happy with you.

Yet if you work with someone that has no capability of continue buying whatever you are selling, well there will no longer be a business, especially if you depend on that client entirely! Make sure you work with successful clients:

how many clients do you have, what are their results, what are their plans for the future, etc?

3. How successful are your stakeholders?

How happy is the community around you with what you do? How much additional values does your business bring to them?

Most of the time businesses focus so much on figures that they forgot what may create their success or their fail: people around them.

Have a look at the community, what is their interest, how can you add something to their life, why shall they be happy to have you as part of their environment?

4. How successful is your footprint, the environmental impact?

We talk a lot about environment these days and yet not enough in relation with business success!

Some businesses consider they have no direct impact on it, so it's not their core preoccupation; some others believe that they do enough to balance some of their negative impact; but let's be honest:

how sustainable can you be if what you do is not respectful to the world you operate in; and this goes way beyond general environment measures; this come within the DNA of the business owner: lead by example, show a different way of doing business with 0 compromise on this one! There is no other way for any successful business to be.

5. How successful is your model?

This more than anything will define your current and future success! What is that you do that makes a difference? How relevant is what you do and for whom?

What is it that your business is bringing to the world? What is your value added? New businesses are created every day, old businesses are still there to provide in a traditional way; look further, think of what it is that you can add to this world and **before thinking about success, think about your impact first!**

"If I were to just try to follow or pretend I was somebody else, it wouldn't be the most true and distinctive version of my highest leadership." Abby Falik ✒

INFLUENCE SELLING:
SERVICE VERSUS SUCKING UP

By Douglas Vermeeren (Canada)

Sales is service, not sucking up.

Sales tactics come in all shapes and sizes. Some work better than others. But even the ones that don't work often show up again and again. Maybe it's because some people just don't know any better.

Maybe in their minds they think it's the right way. Maybe they are doing what they saw someone else do and it appeared **not on the surface to be getting results**.

Habits, Attitudes and ideas are picked up by who we surround ourselves with and who we look up to as teachers. Some of the stuff they teach us works great and some of it is just plain crap.

On this audio I want to have a conversation about one element of sales that I think is really understood in the world today. Often times **people confuse these two things** and label them as one and the same. The truth of the matter is that they couldn't be more distant from each other.

The difference between being

What I am talking about is the difference between being of service and simply sucking up. I want to begin by sharing a few thoughts so you know what I mean by each of these and then share some **major differences between the two philosophies** and the outcomes they are going to create.

These outcomes are important to understand, especially when talking about sucking up. A lot of people think this can help them **speed the process to the sale**. If there's one thing that gets exposed again and again in sales, life, success and almost any other path you want to consider it's that short cuts don't work.

Sucking up is a **short cut**. And although you may think it won't immediately show up or

hurt you in the long run I'm going to show you in a few moments what will happen sooner or later. Short cuts don't work. And sucking up doesn't work either.

I'll start by saying that my goal for you is to have a professional, prosperous career as a sales person. I suspect by now that you have decided to sell something that you believe in and throwing shoddy tactics behind something you see value in is just going to undermine your efforts to success. If you re going to do it, let's get committed to doing it right.

Head straight on to the attributes

I want to begin by talking about sucking up first. Let's get the negative out of the way. Let's talk first about what you don't want to be and then we can head straight on to the **attributes, skills and strategies** that will

make you a winner.

Another way that you have heard people talking about sucking up is to use the phrase **brown nosing, ass kissing** or sometimes people even talk about **being the teachers pet** when you were in school. This was the kid who used to rat on his friends to get the teachers favour, or the kid that **be the goodie** two shoes to win the teachers favour. You may be thinking wait a minute what's wrong with goodie two shoes? Are you saying I have to be the bad ass to make it in sales? Nope.

Sales is all about relationships

I am saying sales is all about relationships. Ask yourself for a minute about that kid who sided with the teacher. How did everyone feel about him or her? How will your clients feel about you if they think you are your bosses pet? If you are in this business to suck up someone is going to **feel that energy** and be repelled by it.

Whether you are sucking up to the boss, your co-workers or even the customer themselves there are a lot of hidden problems that are about to come to light.

When you suck up to a customer you may think that **you are demonstrating loyalty** but they sense that your friendship will shift to whoever has the power. Immediately you are creating distrust.

Before we talk about the results let's share a few of the attributes of sucking up or brown nosing with your customer or others so if you are stumbling a bit in this area you'll be able to recognize it:

Obviously a salesperson who is sucking up will be **insincere, non-authentic, greedy** and out for their own best interest. They are ego driven and even though they may take on the "servant" appearance and place themselves secondary to those who they are sucking up to they are inwardly doing it **for selfish motives**.

They are engaged to **get rather than give**. The simple activity of sucking takes away energy and eventually leaves either one or both people in the situation unsatisfied.

Suck up to their customers

Those that suck up to their customers also often have a hard time exposing the truth. Sometimes to maintain favour they will hide or pass over **things that the customer might object to**, or have concerns with. Their desire to be liked overpowers their need for clarity.

By now if this is you I hope you're recognizing that this won't work in the long term. If it's not you no doubt you've seen a sales person like this before. Maybe they are in your own office. Maybe you can help them by getting them this CD for Christmas. By the way if you got this CD for Christmas.

Don't be mad. **Be thankful** somebody cared enough about you to help you become a better sales person. remember what I was saying a few minutes ago about ego. Ego gets easily offended. Don't be that way. Remember you can *be rich or you can be right*. Chose to learn how to be better and be rich.

Those that suck up will often talk around issues. They have a hard time confronting difficult things. They often spend more time talking than listening because they are coming from a place of insecurity.

Results:

Eventually sucking up creates feelings of resentment. The end result of a sucking up relationship is that one or both of the people will eventually feel that they are **not getting a fair deal** and will feel resentment to the other person. When the sale doesn't happen the sales person **feels betrayed**. If the customer doesn't buy hey feel upset when the "love and

attention" they felt moves on elsewhere.

Sucking up doesn't work.

Celebrities experience this with their fans all the time. I call this experience fan to frustration. I have seen it first hand and even experienced a few times myself. I won't mention any names but a fan and as I mentioned I have done it before too, puts the **celebrity on a pedestal**.

The fan watches the celebrities movies, listens to their records and thence day meets them. As a fan you **subordinate yourself** to them and suck up to them, try and tell them how wonderful they are and then you experience that they are not the same person that you imagined them to be. Now you are no longer a fan, **you are frustrated and upset**. This is the end result that these kinds of relationships create. That's why you can't afford to suck up. You don't need the bad press.

Destroy you own worth

Sucking up also destroys you own worth. As I mentioned before putting yourself in an inferior position to others devalues you. Don't do it. It is not necessary. Besides those you are serving and working with in the sale are expecting you to be the **confident expert**.

Sucking up requires the same amount of energy and work. So rather than trying to put all the effort into being liked let's talk now about how to do it right.

The opposite end of the spectrum is service. If sucking up is on one end, then service is clearly on the other.

<u>Let me explain what I mean by service.</u>

I recently had a customer define service simply this way, 'Service is shocking. Service is shocking." When I asked her what she meant she simply said that service was shocking because when it is **so rare when true service appears** in todays marketplace.

That's an interesting lesson in and of itself. If you want to **stand out from your competition** and be remembered by your customers learn how to be a better servant.

To me service means someone who is **committed to long term relationships**. Not only with the customer, but also the product he is selling. He or she trusts that brand enough that they will learn what they need to know to be of service and they are personally committed to being involved in each interaction and transaction long term.

Service really starts in preparation

Service really starts in preparation. Sucking up is generally done flying by the seat of your pants. Preparation requires a long term vision.

I want to clarify that service and servant are not the same as slave. Slave is actually closer to sucking up. A servant serves because they choose to, they love to, they also get value out of the relationship. A <u>slave has no choice</u>, feels no connection to those they are involved with and **has no loyalty.**

How can you tell if you're a servant? One of the first things that I notice with those who are genuinely there to serve is that they are excited to be there. They love what they do. Others around them can sense that they love what they do. Because they love what they do they come prepare and don't need to be told what to do. They treat all of their relationships customers, boss, co-workers **with dignity and respect.** You can genuinely feel these people care and they are always helpful.

Servants are solution oriented. Where as those brown losers that are suck ups are always complaining. Have you ever had one of those guys privately? Toxic.

Servants are mission based

Servants are mission based seeking those that resonate with the mission. And if you don't resonate with the mission that's okay they will move to others who are more qualified. They won't twist people into being or buying something they are not or do not need.

They seek a fair exchange of value with those that are a good fit. Because of the care they take in this regard they also see a lot more referrals come through their door.

These servant based people are aware that they **need to maintain and manage expectations.** So when they are meeting with clients they share the way things really are. They don't embellish to make a sale and give guarantees that another department can worry about. They prepare the customer for the entire journey so that the experience will be just as good at the end as at the beginning.

I want to be clear that the servant is liked. In fact, often they become far more liked than the one who is sucking up. The reason is simple their relationship is based on value not flashy substitutes.

As I said in the beginning. Sales tactics come in all shapes and sizes.

You are going to see service and you are going to see people sucking up.

Maybe in the past you've done a little bit of both. But there is some great news. Tomorrow is a new day You get to choose which one you will be.

If you choose service let me give you a few suggestions of some things you can do to be effective.

1. Recognize your value. What you bring to the sales relationship is important. You are a valuable asset to the people you are meeting. You are a **valuable asset** to the company you work with. The next step increases your value...that is to increase your value by constantly learning about your products and upgrading your skills.
2. **GROW YOUR VALUE** -As you upgrade yourself through product knowledge and levelling up your life and skills you can't help but grow in value. A few years ago I had a chance to interview a young man who for three years in a row had won his car dealerships award as the **most distinguished and successful sales person.** He told me the interesting story of how he grew into that position and it was quite simple. He spent time everyday adding significantly to his skills and product knowledge. Every time someone walked onto the lot to buy a car and there was a question the customers were sent to him. He was **splitting nearly every commission** that came through the door because the other guys just weren't prepared enough to answer the questions. Naturally those people who interacted with him **had a great experience** and sent their friends too. So basically he was getting all his own customers, plus a half commission on almost all of the other deals coming through and then the referrals on top of that. There's high value in become the smartest guy in the room.
3. Give your expertise without expectation - This one is important. Too often those who suck up expect that if you kiss your rear end you owe them something. The customer senses it. And if you're doing it to the boss, trust me he knows why you're doing it. And if you think it's working out - trust me the end of the story may surprise you. **Either he or you will eventually be frustrated.** There's an old saying that he who kisses ass eventually gets chapped lips. Needless to say those who serve without expectation are never disappointed. In fact, they are often surprised. I have personally experienced times when I have been helpful to someone who I assumed **was not ready to buy** and then they returned and became one of **my best repeat customers.** Your helpfulness creates a loyalty that reappears when you least expect it. I am also a firm believer that karma finds its way back to everyone. And givers get. Help others with their needs and your needs get met. I also find that helping those in your own office succeed eventually comes back to you as well. I was speaking with a financial planner not too long ago who was doing really well in his office. It seemed like promotion after promotion came his way, not to mention all the contest he won. When I asked him the secret to his success he told me I just stop and help everyone I can. His supervisors saw how helpful he was to others and promotion after promotion started showing up. He was able to take others higher and grow his own business. I am sure that if was doing that to be seen and recognized he would have been passed over.
4. **Get prepared and stay prepared.** I am not just speaking about skills and product knowledge that I mentioned above I am know talking about how you show up. On time, prepared and ready to go. Certainly first impressions are important, but so is **consistency.** Your customers want to be able to trust you and when they see that your meetings with them are important they will respond.
5. Stay present. Often times I will invite sales people to the house because I like to watch their presentations for my own learning. A few years ago my wife and I invited an air filter salesman into our house and he was unprepared. The presentation was a disaster as he kept returning to his car to retrieve gear he had forgotten. We talked a moment ago about being prepared. He missed that one. But this moment is really about being present. Here he missed it entirely. This guys phone would buzz and he **paused the presentation to reply** to several of these texts and even took a phone call while he made us wait. I just joking said, "You wife must be on her way to the hospital to have a baby." He laughed and said no just so friends wanting to hook up tonight. It was a mess. Needless to say stay present. True servants **stay present** with those they are with.
6. Maybe this final one is the most important and if you do this I believe all the other stuff will come together. *Here we go: simply be genuine.* When you are real people feel it. Be interested, be sincere, provide value, when you complement make it legit. Real people get real results.

Service beats sucking up every time.

Don't sell yourself short. Get committed right now to offering the highest level of service you can and becoming a true value to those you serve. They will thank you for it and so will your future self.

Life is too short to create substitutes and short cuts that you will later regret or have to repair. Do it right the first time.

↗

ANIMATION NOW AND THEN

By Phil Roman (USA)

From the early 1900's, people have been **attracted to animation** for the

novelty of **watching drawings come to life**. Some of the earliest pioneers in animation were Emile Cohl from France with "Fantasmagorie", Lotte Reiniger from Germany, a pioneer in silhouette animation, and Winsor McCay, who animated "Gertie the Dinosaur" in 1914. Those early efforts inspired other animators. Eventually, studios popped up producing characters such as Felix the Cat and Betty Boop, which struck a cord in people's heart. Their popularity spread worldwide. Some characters became more known than many movie stars.

As the animation business grew, animated theatrical shorts were introduced before the main movie by the major studios like Warner Bros. and MGM, with characters such as Tom & Jerry, Mickey Mouse and Bugs Bunny, whose popularity continues to this day.

One of the early main forces behind animation was **Walt Disney**. In 1928 he produced "Steamboat Willie", the first cartoon with sound. It was very well received by the

audience and encouraged him to do ore shorts. He was producing Mickey Mouse and Donald Duck shorts as well as the "Silly Symphonies". These shorts helped Disney push to limits of what could be done with animation, as their quality was improving tremendously. By the mid 1930's had decided to produce a full-length animated motion picture, "Snow White and the seven Dwarfs", which was an immediate success.

Through the years, the technology of producing animation has changed a lot.

When I started working, animation was as low-tech as you can imagine. A **pencil**, a **piece of paper**, and **your imagination** were all it took.

Traditional animation was eventually succeeded by today's computer animation. In 1995, Pixar pioneered Computer Generated-animation with "Toy Story". It was a big success and other studios like Dreamworks and Disney transitioned to CG-animation. The technique ensures that films are produced faster, thus allowing that animation is not only used for theatrical

features and TV series but also for commercials and web series.

The audience reacted positively to the new look. Now, Brands, too, are producing animated videos using technologies such as Virtual Reality and 360 Degree technology to please their audience and build a platform for their products.

Back in my day, animators were called "Pencil-pushers", I call today's computer animators "Pixel-pushers".

What started out as theatrical novelty, has bloomed into a multi-billion Dollar business. According to market research, the **Global Animation Market** is projected to Reach **US$ 270 Billion by 2020**.

The demand for animation and gaming has expanded with the increase in broadcasting by cable and satellite TV, availability of low-cost internet, and streaming on mobile devices. The rapid advancement of technology has made animation available to the masses, and the industry has become one of the fastest growing segments in the global media and

entertainment market.

Global consumers have a growing appetite for high-definition visual experiences with engaging visual effects and realistic animation and studios are including more animation into films. Animation, content is being consumed not only on Netflix and Amazon, but also on YouTube and Twitter. With growing internet presence and access to multimedia devices, customers are spending **more time streaming digital content.** Thus, **streaming video** is the fastest growing segment distribution channel for animation.

However, some things have not changed with technology: the ideas for stories, character design and story telling. You still need the **human imagination.**

About the Author

A true success story, six-time Emmy-winner and Winsor McCay Award. Recipient, **Phil Roman** has animated, directed and produced animated series, and feature films for over five decades. He has worked with legends such as **Walt Disney, Chuck Jones**, Joe Barbera, and Bill Melendez. He was a lead animator on "How the Grinch Stole Christmas" as well as on "The Dot and the Line", which **won an Oscar**. He also directed several of "The Peanuts" specials.

The animation studio he founded, Film Roman, produced "The Simpsons", "Bobby's World", "Mad Max", "The Mask" and "King of the Hill" for 20th Century Fox and MTV, as well as the "Garfield" animated television

specials and subsequent series, "Garfield and Friends". Phil Roman also directed the first eleven of the twelve primetime Garfield animated television specials, and "Tom and Jerry: The Movie", his first theatrical feature, alongside friends Joe Barbera and Henry Mancini.

Phil Roman is still actively involved in animation. He is consulting on various animation projects and is always on the lookout for new challenges. To this day, his motto is:

"You have to believe in yourself and never give up. There will be rejection and times when you think it's over. But never stop dreaming, and dream big, because dreams do come true."- Phil Roman

MOISTURE FOR COMFORT WHILE FLYING

By Aldrin-David Verburgt (The Netherlands)

The world has become significantly smaller. We are not limited by our zip codes anymore, which leads the entrepreneurs of today to expand their horizons and explore new fields to boost their business successfully, miles and miles (or kilometers) from home.

By planes, trains and automobiles we travel around the world. Exploring new cultures; people and new countries are getting more accessible. Regardless if the reason for travel is a well-deserved holiday or perhaps you

travel for business.

But travelling takes more time than 'just a commute'. Did you ever wonder why you may look tired after a trip, even after 6-8 hours of sleep?

Especially when you find yourself on a long (international) flight, 5 hours or more, your skin probably feels like as if it's tight or starts to 'pull'. This is a sign of dehydration, and it's even noticeable on shorter domestic flights.

When you are on a business trip, you don't want to arrive with dehydrated, dry looking or even worse, a flaky skin that makes you look untidy, tired and worn out.

What you do want to make sure of is to emphasize on healthy, hydrated and radiant skin.

This equals to a professional, successful and attractive image, just like a custom fit suit and polished shoes do. Your message is absolutely

important, the very same goes for the messenger!

When you work in an environment or situation that's constantly exposed to dry air (no regular access to fresh air), like airplanes, trains and offices it can have a more dramatic longer lasting uncomfortable effect on our skin. This might be a point of some concern for people who have a career in the corporate world where the professionals constantly work indoors in heated and air-conditioned spaces.

Here are some tips to prevent any discomfort of experiencing dehydration of your skin while flying.

1. Use an extra moisture-based shower gel in the morning.
2. Moisturise your skin with a body lotion, body cream or body oil.
3. Apply a daily moisturiser in the morning and evening.
4. Use a moisture serum underneath your skincare to prevent dehydration
5. Apply skincare with extra lipids (edition skincare: for dry skin)
6. Apply hand cream throughout the day.
7. Apply a lip balm for the sensitive skin of your lips.
8. You can bring a moisturiser to reapply this to your skin for more comfort.
9. Moisture sprays to refreshen and comfort the skin.
10. Drink plenty of water throughout the day.

Important is to moisture inside out! Drink minimal 1,5- 2 litres of water a day.

On your next flight, before takeoff, take a moment to refresh your face with a moisture spray, apply your hand cream and lip balm while the plane taxies to the runway. It literally only takes one minute! Once up in the air feel free to ask the flight attendant for an extra glass of water while you read the latest issue of Business Booster Today Magazine.

Remember, you can only make a first impression once ... So, make it impeccable!

You are the expert and know how to play the game in your field of expertise. Dress well, be confident and let your healthy and radiant looking skin 'do the talking'.

START-UPS NEED THE RIGHT GUIDANCE

By Christian Bartsch (Germany)

Many new companies in the technology field suffer from a massive cashflow issue as they focus far too long on building a perfect product or service. During this time more agile competitors will overtake them and drive them out of business.

In order to avoid running out of funds, these tech startups need a business coaching that is not based on standard recipies. Having founded several businesses and experienced the value of the business coach that helped me

take my business to the next level, i do recommend to use of that.

Is it enough to have a coach?

No, you need to have a mentor that is willing to share with you his or her business experience. This will usually be an entrepreneur with more than 20 years business experience. In some cases you will find a former CEO for a subsidiary or major corporation that did not own the business but

restructured the business.

Founders of technology companies are great analytic people. They can program software, develop hardware or come up with the most innovative chemical formula that replaces outdated manufacturing methods.

Schools and universities do not provides us with the necessary sales and new business development skills. These skills need to be learned outside of the outdated education

TO GET CASHFLOW COMING IN

system. Learning how to close a deal or how to create the first pitch of a product to the first corporate beta client .. that needs guidance.

Other skills you will develop as you go. Each time you have a client on the phone, you will learn my doing. It will be painful to be rejected but eventually you will know your pitch so well, that you do not think about it. It automatically comes with its customized structure out of you in response to the individual client's comments.

Having coached several business owners in Germany, UK, USA and Canada, I noticed that there was a lack of clarity how to get to a positive cash flow. Then i remembered having several check lists for our shipping, travels and flights.

That is why I then decided to reduce the complexity and to create easy to follow cheat sheets. That would make it easier for my clients to stay on track in between the coaching sessions we have. If you are

interested, send me an email at info@gainyoursucess.com ✐

AIR CARGO MARKETS HAVE RECOVERED - MARKET OVERVIEW -

By Udo Bartsch (Germany)

After several years of weak demand and a lagging recovery of the global economy, the air cargo traffic has fully recovered in 2017. It grew by more than 10%. This is more than twice the rate of the long-term average. This was due to three factors:

1. Global economic expansion

2. Increasing industrial production

3. World trade growth

As you will remember, the air cargo traffic greatly outpaced the capacity growth in the last two years, absorbing the excess capacity. The results were rising load factors and improved profitability.

After the strong growth in 2017, the global freight growth has moderated in 2018. Many indicators show that the air cargo market is fundamentally well positioned to maintain the growth momentum. Strong growth is expected to come from e-commerce, time-sensitive perishables as well as high-value commodities including computers, consumer electronics, and pharmaceuticals which are the fastest growing trade sectors around the world.

In 2018 the air cargo transport measured in revenue tonne-kilometres is estimated to grow by about 4 percent. The cargo revenue is expected exceed $100 billion.

In the last two decades, the evolution of Internet technology has led to the explosive growth of e-commerce. E-commerce takes a growing share of the air cargo market. The market size varies by country. It is driven by China, with approximately €1.1 trillion, the Asia-Pacific region, defined as South Asia and East Asia, which is the largest e-commerce in the world.

The second largest e-commerce market in the world is the United States. Sales reached to more than $ 450 billion in e-commerce sales in 2017, i.e. 16% RTK more than in 2016. (RTK: revenue tonne-kilometre)

World air cargo outlook

The world air cargo traffic is expected to grow in the next years by 4 - 4,5% for the next 20 years, Asia will continue to lead the world in average annual air cargo growth.

Expected growth

China: 6,3%

intra-East Asia: 5,8%

This is supported by fast growing economies and growing middle classes. The East Asia-North America and Europe-East Asia markets will grow slightly faster than the world average growth rate. The Latin America and Middle East markets connected to Europe and North America will grow slightly faster than the world average growth rate. Less optimistic is the outlook for the trade flows between North America and Europe with expected growth rate below the world average.

Importance of freighters

Air cargo represents just about 1% of global trade by tonnage. Looking at the value of the traded goods using air freight transport, the picture looks quite different. Air cargo represents more than 35% of the global trade by value. This is because air cargo is transporting goods which are desperately required at the destination, e.g. machinery, computing account, spare parts, perishable goods. Also computing equipment and electrical equipment as well as account for the highest share of air borne trade tonnage.

There are 2 options for air cargo transport: a) dedicated freighters and b) passenger aircraft lower holds. Each alternative has its advantage. Freighters are particularly well

suited for transporting high value goods, because they provide highly controlled transport direct routing, reliability and a unique capacity consideration.

With the introduction of a new generation of widebody passenger aeroplanes with larger lower-hold capacity quite a number of airlines are combining cargo transportation with passenger operation to capitalize on additional revenue opportunities. Belly cargo space offers unique value on non-cargo routes by feeding dedicated freighter networks and providing new business opportunities.

However, while lower-hold capacity in widebody airplanes serving long-haul missions has increased by nearly 6 percent in the last 5 years, several parameters can limit the cargo operations in passenger aircraft. The reduced height of the lower deck can limit the volumes. From the network standpoint, freighter routes are highly concentrated on relatively few trade lanes, especially in the world´s two largest trade routes, East Asia-North America and East Asia-Europe. In contrast, passenger networks are much broader and often include destinations where cargo demand is minimal. The difference in

passenger and cargo traffic distribution explains the considerable load factor difference in belly space and freighters, which average approximately 30 percent and 70 percent respectively. In addition, range restrictions on fully loaded passenger aircraft and limited service to major cargo airports make freighter operations essential. For these structural reasons, freighters are forecast to carry more than half of the world´s air cargo for the next 20 years.

Express carriers continue to operate substantial freighter fleets, flying more than half of the widebody freighters and generating 43 percent of air cargo industry revenues in 2017.

Low cost carriers (LCC) have increased their share of air cargo traffic, particularly in Southeast Asia. However, even with fast growth in the passenger markets and the recent surge in low-cost long-haul development, LCCs are still estimated to carry less than 2 percent of air cargo traffic.

Freighter fleet outlook

The air cargo traffic is expected to double in the next 20 years and the world freighter fleet

will grow by more than 70 percent, from the current 1,870 to 3,260 airplanes. Growing demand for regional express services in fast-developing economies will boost the standard-body share of the freighter fleet from 37 percent today to 39 percent. Like the current fleet, the 1,170 standard-body freighter deliveries forecast in the next two decades will be converted passenger airplanes.

In the next 20 years, 2,650 freighters are forecast to be delivered, with approximately half replacing retiring airplanes and the reminder expanding the fleet to meet projected growth. More than 63 percent of deliveries will be freighter conversions, of which nearly 70 percent will be standard-body passenger airplanes. A projected 980 new production freighters, valued at $280 billion, will be delivered, of which more than 50 percent will be in the large-freighter category, such as the 747 Freighter and 777 Freighter. The competition between Airbus and Boeing has been characterised as a duopoly in the large jets, however all orders for the A380 freighter variant have been cancelled. ✈

BMW X7 - THE OFFROAD POWERHOUSE

By Christian Bartsch (Germany)

The BMW X7

The BMW X7 is the first car to fuse the **presence, exclusivity and spaciousness** of a luxury model with the agile and versatile driving properties expected of a **Sports Activity Vehicle** (SAV).

BMWs continued Growth

When I reflect upon the fact that over 20 years ago during my business training at the BMW HQ in Munich the first Z3 was introduced, the BMW Group has been growing its product pallete.

During my training I was part of the Rover project. Having to translate parts lists for the planed joint purchase project. It was an exiting time as the **diversity of the team** would show a young person how much power you can gain from a multinational team.

The X7 is a massive vehicle that has an impressive presence. It is so ahead of time in comparison to other competitor's products. The **advanced electronics and design** will positively surprise you.

Let me introduce to you this **powerhouse on 4 wheels**.

The BMW Vision iNext

The BMW Vision iNext marks the dawn of a new era in driving pleasure. This is the first time the strategic innovation fields of **Automated Driving, Connectivity, Electrification and Services** have been fully integrated in a single vehicle, which lends them **visual expression** with its future-focused design (D+ACES).

The areas of action the BMW Group has identified to ensure the company's sustained growth also include an **increased presence in the luxury segment**. The current offensive in this vehicle class is clearly evidenced by the new BMW X7.

Setting its sights on the future of driving pleasure the BMW Vision iNext.

The BMW Vision iNEXT showcases the possibilities offered by **autonomous mobility** in the not too distant future. It demonstrates solutions designed first and foremost to inject fresh energy, all while focusing clearly on a **human-centric approach**. The production model based on the BMW Vision iNext will serve as the company's new technological flagship. According to BMW the first vehicles will be rolling off the assembly line at BMW Plant Dingolfing in **2021**.

Adopting the dimensions and proportions of a modern BMW Sports Activity Vehicle (SAV), the BMW Vision iNEXT presents an **authoritative figure**. Its pioneering character shines through in its clearly sculpted forms and surfaces. The car's front is dominated by the large BMW kidney grille. With no combustion engine to require cooling, the grille is blanked off and serves as an "**intelligence panel**" housing various sensors.

Slim headlights provide a modern take on BMW's signature **four-eyed front** silhouette. The BMW Vision iNEXT displays the powerful, **robust stance** of a modern BMW SAV when viewed from the side, while its functional two-box proportions and long

roofline hint at the generous space inside. Its long wheelbase and short overhangs, meanwhile, give the car's outline a dynamic powerhouse. Two large opposing doors and the **absence of B-pillars** ensure supreme ease of access to the car's interior, which takes the form of a snug and fashionably furnished "living space" on wheels.

New dimension in luxurious driving

The addition of the BMW X7 to the Bavarian premium carmaker's model portfolio opens up a **brand new dimension in luxurious driving** pleasure. The newest and also largest representative of the BMW X family blends **lavish presence, functionality and room-comfort** with the agile and supremely assured driving properties customers would expect from a Sports Activity Vehicle (SAV).

BMW's new design language brings the **modern elegance characteristic** of the brand's luxury-segment models to the exterior of the BMW X7, while also giving it a distinctly self-assured air.

Up to **three seat-rows or as a six-seater** with comfort seats offer remarkable levels of space, sophisticated design and *exclusive equipment*

features combine to give the cabin a truly luxurious feel.

Power under the bonnet

The line-up of engines for the brand's first luxury SAV comprises a **petrol V8** (not available in Europe), a six-cylinder in-line petrol unit and a pair of six-cylinder in-line diesels. All engines team up with an **eight-speed Steptronic transmission** and the BMW xDrive intelligent all-wheel-drive system. This ensures an unforgetable drivning experience.

Offroad & Executive Drive

The BMW X7 comes equipped as standard with **two-axle air suspension and Adaptive suspension** with electronically controlled dampers. Depending on the engine variant, customers also have the option of an M Sport differential and an Off-Road package, not to mention the **Executive Drive Pro** chassis system with active roll stabilisation.

The BMW X7 sticks to the formula of off-road ability combined with *impressive driving comfort and agile road handling* for

which its SAV models are renowned, courtesy of advanced powertrain and chassis technology.

The progressive luxury epitomised by the BMW X7 is further underlined by the broad spread of **cutting-edge driver assistance systems** on offer. The Driving Assistant Professional package (including the Steering and lane control assistant) and the Parking Assistant with Reversing Assistant most vividly embody the latest advances towards automated driving.

Also to be found on the list of standard equipment is the BMW Live Cockpit Professional, comprising a fully digital instrument cluster and Control Display each with a screen diagonal of 12.3 inches.

Plus, the new BMW Operating System 7.0 enables optimised **multimodal operation** using the iDrive Controller, the **touchscreen display**, the steering wheel buttons, or voice and **gesture control**.

Inside Experience

The new BMW X7 isn't shy. Charismatic design features make it stand out, from the new one-piece kidney grille to the expressive lines that flow elegantly to the **eye-catching**

3D L-shaped LED taillights. Add to this the brilliant 21" light alloy wheels, and curious eyes won't know where to look.

Sitting in the new BMW X7 simply feels different. It still evokes that unique BMW feeling with its Individual Extended Merino leather upholstery and **dynamic ambient lighting**; however, thanks to the Panorama Glass Sunroof, which comes as standard, and the new optional 6-seat configuration with two captain-style comfort seats in the second row, it also has the power to surprise the senses.

Enjoy a Massage

The standard Comfort seats for driver and front passenger in the BMW X7 immerse you in an overwhelming feeling of relaxation and comfort. The Massage function, available as optional equipment, for the driver and front passenger helps to improve the physical well-being by stimulating or relaxing certain muscle groups. There are eight massage programmes dedicated to different parts of the body. There are three intensity levels. Exclusively available as part of the Premium package.

Wheel Design

At 22 inches, the optional light alloy Multi-spoke style 757 wheels, exclusively available for xDrive4i and xDrive3d models, are among the **largest wheels** in the portfolio and thus radiate an unmistakable presence when viewed from the side. Finished in Bicolour, they look particularly noble.

Overall Conclusion

The vehicle body looks **more powerful, refined and luscious** with the lavish surfaces without losing the sportiness that is typical to BMW.

Especially in their large and particularly luxurious vehicles, BMW attaches great importance to a marked appearance and the maximum possible **feel-good factor** in the interior. It's about freedom – and the feeling of being at home in a BMW.

The design has to arouse strong emotions while expressing the highest quality and durability at the same time. In order to be able to spend **every moment intensely, full of meaning and beauty**. The X7 designer team have achieved to succeed at this massive challenge they set for the design of this new BMW. ✐

POLLUTION ON THE WESTERN FRONT

By Christian Bartsch (Germany)

As we move to the many different 100- year celebrations, we must be aware that there is a massive problem in the heart of Europe. It has been sitting there for over 100 years. This problem started in 1914 and did not end in 1918.

Yes, it is more than a 100-years since the 3 key nations fighting at the western front. We often read or see movies about the World War 1 battles around Verdun. Reality is that even after 100 years not all bodies have been recovered in certain areas of the former front lines. These areas have been marked as hazardous for humans to enter.

The toxic levels of pollution due to the ammunition, the different poisons that the involved armies used to try to win a few meters ground are still there deep in the fields and forests.

Even the threat posed by the ammunition that is on the surface and below is so serious that wanderers could suffer life threatening injuries should the tread on, near or even pick up such ammunition. You would think that even with all the clean up after the 2nd World war the fields and forests would be safe.

The "Zone Rouge" is a chain of non-contiguous areas throughout northeastern France that the French government isolated after World War I. This zone was declared because of the vast amounts of human and animal remains and millions of items of unexploded ammunition contaminating the land.

Soils were heavily polluted by lead, mercury, chlorine and arsenic. The various dangerous gases and acids used to attack enemy lines also remain in the ground and contaminate the vegetation. The area was also littered with ammunition depots and chemical plants. The Sécurité Civile agency estimates that at the current rate 300 to 700 more years will be needed to clean the area completely.

These areas were often coined as "No Mans land". In World War I, no man's land often ranged from several hundred yards to in some cases less than 10 yards. These areas were heavily defended by machine guns, mortars and artillery. The massive amount of ammunition being fired across the lines is still to be found just 15 cm below the ground surface.

On both side riflemen exchanged bullets from machine guns, trying to kill anybody trying to look out into the enemy lines. Even inside the trenches they were not safe as the trench could not spare the men from the odd cross-bat shot. This area was often extensively cratered, riddled with barbed wire, and rudimentary improvised land mines. Often wounded soldiers would not be able to make it through the hail of bullets, explosions and flames back into their own trenches. The area was sometimes contaminated by chemical weapons.

Despite the condition of the shells, they remain very dangerous.

The French Département du Déminage (Department of Mine Clearance) recovers about 900 tons of unexploded munitions every year. In the last 75 years approximately 630 French clearers have died handling unexploded munitions. Two French clearers died handling munitions outside Vimy (France) in 1998. Over 20 members of Belgian Explosive Ordnance Disposal (DOVO) have died disposing of First World War munitions. This special unit was formed in 1919.

Unfortunately, even until today civilian deaths are also common. In just the area around Ypres, 260 people have been killed and 535 have been injured by unexploded munitions since the end of the First World War. Shells containing poisonous gas remain viable and will corrode and release their gas content. Close to five percent of the shells fired during the First World War contained poisonous gas

and ordnance disposal experts continue to suffer burns from mustard gas shells that were split open.

This is why the German, French, Belgium and British government must provide more funding and resources so that the loss of lives and the damage to the environment is rapidly decreased. In a world where we can build, drones to fly and robots to play tennis there must be a greater emphasis to provide modern technology to as well reduce the work risks to the brave men and women who are trying to handle the left overs of the First World War.

The key nations involved in the greatest types of pollution were Germany, Britain and France. Those actively most hurt by the long-term damage are the French and the Belgium nations.

The first use of poison gas occurred during the Second Battle of Ypres (22 April – 25 May 1915). The French attack on German trenches using gas and flame throwers in Flanders is even recorded on photography. The German and the British troops also attacked each other with all sorts of gas. Same happened on the eastern front between Russian and German troops. The number of casualties on all sides due to this terrible weapon is way above 1.3 million. After the battles the results of the mustard gas were visible in the many poppy flowers. The poppy flower is the symbol of remembrance in many countries.

Of course, you could argument that the use of such terrible weapons was a war crime. The truth is that all sides committed these crimes. The use of chemical weapons in warfare was in direct violation of the 1899 Hague Declaration Concerning Asphyxiating Gases and the 1907 Hague Convention on Land Warfare, which prohibited their use.

HOW TO STAY SANE IN A SOMETIMES INSANE BUSINESS WORLD (PART 1)

By Marina Kotze (South Africa)

As a mental health care practitioner and entrepreneur, I am fully aware of the daily struggles, hardships, pressure and stress that business owners are facing and have to deal with. "Doing" life, business, family, relationships and the combination of everything is taxing and demanding. I totally get it. What I also get is the lack of certain skillsets that, sadly, many business owners have in terms of looking after themselves and nurturing their quality of life. Just as one is able to acquire and learn the skills to become a successful business owner, we can also learn the ins and outs of looking after our physical, emotional and mental health.

Many people have heard about the concept of mental health and even loosely throw the term around in various conversations, but do they actually know what "mental health" is and what it entails? We can't really integrate anything effectively in our lives if we do not truly understand it; if we have a concept of something, we can understand its function and purpose. With mental illness on a rapid rise in today's modern society all over the world, it is of vital importance for all of us to gain a thorough understanding of mental health and wellbeing. We can't look after our businesses, our bank accounts, employees and everyone else around us, without prioritizing our own mental health as vitally important. So, let us get down to learn what we can about cultivating personal mental health.

"Your health is your wealth." – Marina Kotzé

The obvious question is, what IS mental health? In a nutshell, mental health is like an overall umbrella that consists of a variety of components. These components are a person's cognitive abilities, thought processes, emotional functioning, communication, motivation and drive, interpersonal relationships, self-esteem, activities of daily living and personal management, leisure participation, coping skills, and work abilities. In addition, attention should be given to *how*, to what *extent*, and the *quality* of how a person is able function in each of these components. During my years of clinical practice in adult psychiatry, I have come to realize a common theme amongst working with my clients and patients – that there are very specific key aspects of their mental health that are affected and where there is a

definite lack of knowledge and skills in those areas. These deficits run like a golden thread through the lives of many people – even the general population and the business community are no exception. In my opinion, these key aspects are **insight**, **judgement** (both of which are aspects of a person's cognition), **coping skills** and setting **boundaries**. Let me introduce each individually and explain some more:

INSIGHT

I am starting with the trickiest one here… Insight is definitely not for the faint hearted, so to speak. It is often a very tough topic to engage with, as it entails facing our demons and learning how to deal with it. Remember, gaining insight is a skill which can be gained. This should give you hope to learn and grow on your journey towards optimum mental health. There are various stages of insight which vary between having no insight at all, to having some awareness, to having fully developed emotional insight – which is like summiting Mount Everest in the world of insight. As you can imagine, having full emotional insight is the ultimate goal in learning and growing in insight! The ones who posses this treasure and attribute are people who take FULL responsibility for their lives, actions and behaviors. They are emotionally mature and definitely people to look up to in society.

So then, where and how does one start developing insight? Developing insight starts with gaining knowledge and information on mental health. Reading mainstream educational books on human thoughts, emotions and behavior is a good way to start gaining intellectual insight. Reading up and talking to mental health care professionals on specific diagnoses, signs and symptoms is a step further on developing intellectual insight.

In our daily business practice, gaining and having *intellectual insight* should be an integral part of our daily habits. For example, stress is a common occurrence in the business community and having intellectual insight would mean to understand what stress is, the causes of it in your life, the signs and symptoms that you experience, and how to treat it. Other examples of commonalities within the business community are anxiety, depression and burn-out. Learn about these topics and any other topic that may apply to

you, a colleague, an employee and anybody else you care about.

Gaining *emotional insight* will then be the next step. Emotional insight is being aware and understanding how your behavior affects other people. It is also about being aware of your own emotions, how to effectively regulate it, and the role emotions play in your own behavior and then eventually, once again, the effect it has on those around you. One of the best ways to gaining and developing emotional insight is to get and ask for feedback from your support system, friends, loved ones, colleagues, coaches and therapists. It is then important to be open to receive those feedback, give it a good portion of your thoughts, and make the necessary changes and adjustments. Changed behavior is the result of developed emotional insight, which comes down to how we make other people feel, how we treat others, and our attitude towards business, life and relationships.

JUDGEMENT

Part of the "cognition family", judgement plays a crucial role in making decisions, in planning what steps to take, how to interact in certain situations, and what relationships to pursue. Judgement is where one is weighing up certain factors, for example, the pros versus cons, the positives versus negatives, worse case versus best case scenario, and past experiences versus new experiences. Poor judgement often, if not always, lead to poor decision making, and poor decision making to poor results. In a business setting, it may imply that poor decisions have been made based on poor judgement as a result of a lack of information, facts and figures. That is why proper investigations and research on a particular topic or business endeavor is so important, which will allow one to weigh up all the options before a decision is made. Good judgement prevents "thumb sucking" and empowers one to make calculated risks. Good judgement is also the watchman, so to speak, in making over-hasty decisions. Where investments, new relationships, new business endeavors and even a new direction for a company are involved, good, rational and sound judgement is key in making sure decisions are healthy and constructive.

Again, there are different types of judgement – anything from concrete, abstract, to social,

critical and automatic judgement. Without giving too much detail on each, I would rather give an example or two of each within a business setting.

Concrete judgement pertains to anything on a concrete, tangible level, and something that is measurable when applicable. For example, for us ladies, it would mean to use the right amount of make-up applied in the most appropriate way for a certain setting or situation. For a man, it might be applying the right amount of hair gel to style his hair in the best possible way.

Abstract judgement is where emotions and behavior come into play. For example, when you are in a very important business meeting and you urgently have to excuse yourself, good abstract judgement will help you to handle the situation appropriately and in a professional manner. Another example is in the use of good manners and etiquette – something that never goes out of fashion, by the way – we might possess the know-how and skills of good manners and etiquette, but how to apply it in the best appropriate way in a variety of situations is where good and sound abstract judgement comes in very handy.

Social judgement is about how one perceives, approaches and behaves in social settings. It is about being aware of the social and cultural setting you find yourself in and then making the necessary adjustments for appropriate social contact and engagement. Social judgement is also about the manner and way in which you present yourself to others in social gatherings and meetings, which is very common in the business world. An everyday example would be wearing the appropriate attire to match the business occasion.

Critical judgement indicates a situation where a problem of a critical nature presents itself and one has to put careful thought into it as to how to best and most appropriately handle the situation. It may also entail an emergency situation, and even a life and death scenario. Higher order thinking comes into play here, where the critical situation is viewed from all angles, all possible options are weighed up against one another, where a variety of expert opinions are gathered, and at the end the best possible decision(s) are made to ensure a minimum loss in that specific situation. In a business scenario, for example, it may be where an employee has acted illegally against the CEO of a company – where it is of such a serious nature that the future of the company might be jeopardized – which has been brought under the attention of the CEO, and now, what the CEO will do with that information and how the CEO will respond depend greatly upon his or her critical judgement abilities.

Automatic judgement is as simple as that – where an action has been done so many times that eventually it becomes automatic and second nature, and no extra thought is necessary to put into it. Driving a manual motor vehicle becomes second nature and automatic judgement is used when changing gears. In the business world, knowledge about people and their behavior is important. Therefore, to "sum up" people and to have a general impression about people helps tremendously in business relationships. As a skilled businessman and woman, it eventually becomes second nature to "sum up" people and automatic judgement kicks in on how to engage and build business relationships with people.

Keeping these four aspects in mind in your daily business practice, will greatly assist in making your personal mental health a top priority. Just as one invests in the health and growth of one's business, one should invest in one's own mental health and development. Success should not only be worked for, but the fruit of all the hard work, long hours, sacrifices and dedication should also be enjoyed. Success should also not be achieved at the cost of one's health. Achieve great success, while keeping in mind that along your business journey, your health and mental wellness should be kept intact. No dollar is ever worth your sanity! ✒

PROPERTY SOURCING PROFITS:

By John Stokoe (United Kingdom)

STEP THREE: How do I present the deal to investors?

So, you've found your first deal. The numbers stack up and your offer has been accepted. Now comes the most important part, sourcing process—packaging up your deal into an investment-grade opportunity that you can monetize. This quite simply involves transcribing the amazing deal you've secured on to paper (or a digital version), in an easy to understand format, so that an investor can review it and decide whether to purchase the deal.

Remember, this is your opportunity to market and sell your deal to an investor so it's important that it's packaged effectively. You should ensure it is well presented, with clear calculations, and that the due diligence and creative opportunities associated with this property deal are well explained and substantiated. As a litmus test of sorts, it's always good to have someone who has no understanding of the deal look over it for you. If they have any questions, you probably have a gap in your explanation.

"When it comes to presenting a deal, I have one simple rule – if this deal was on a piece of a paper and was picked up by someone in the street, they should be able to easily understand the opportunity, how the numbers work and have confidence in the deal based on the supporting information provided." - John Stokoe

Your Source Pack should contain:

The Property

Provide a brief description of the property, including all important details—the type of property, number of bedrooms, number of bathrooms, size of garden, parking facilities etc. Describe the current condition of the property, what work needs doing and any creative ways you might add value. Where possible, include photos to give your potential buyer a better idea of what they're purchasing—no one has ever dated someone without a profile picture! Finally, describe possible exit strategies for the property; for example, as a buy-to-let it cash-flows £280pcm, as a flip it offers a profit of £11,000.

The Area

PACKAGE THE DEAL

Next, provide a description of the area in which the property is situated, including the distance to local schools and amenities, any notable employers or towns within commuting distance and any local transport links. This is your opportunity to demonstrate this property is suitable for multiple individuals; from the single professional commuting to work, to first time buyers looking for their family home. Be sure to include the following details:

Local Schools |Transport links | Developments | Distance to town centre |Local amenities

The Numbers

To provide a property investor with the details they need to decide whether a deal works for them, the numbers have to be simple and easy to follow. Be sure to include market comparable to substantiate any estimates or

assumptions. We have continually refined our packaging criteria and now include all of the following:

FLIP:

Purchase Price | Expected Re-sale Price | Refurb Costs | Entry & Exit Legal Costs | Stamp Duty | Broker Fee | Source Fee | 6 Months Bills & Mortgage | Estate Agent Commission

RENTAL:

Asking Price | Agreed Sale Price | Done-Up Value Estimate | Refurb Costs | Flip Profit | Cash Flow @ 3%| Cash Flow

For more details on this process we run a Sourcing academy :
https://www.sourcemyproperty.com/academy/